YORK
COURSES

A COURSE IN FIVE SESSIONS WRITTEN BY DAVID WINTER
ACCOMPANYING CD/AUDIOTAPE AND TRANSCRIPT AVAILABLE

GLIMPSES OF GOD

HOPE FOR TODAY'S WORLD

TRANSCRIPT for
GLIMPSES OF GOD
Hope for today's world

This transcript accompanies the
CD/audiotape for the course entitled
Glimpses of God - Hope for today's
world. The words spoken on the
CD/audiotape are set out in this
transcript booklet.

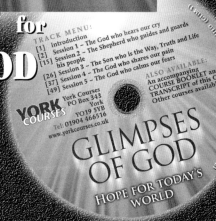

TRACK MENU:
[1] Introduction
[2] Session 1 – The God who hears our cry
[15] Session 2 – The Shepherd who guides and guards
        his people
[26] Session 3 – The Son who is the Way, Truth and Life
[37] Session 4 – The God who shares our pain
[49] Session 5 – The God who calms our fears

YORK
COURSES

York Courses
PO Box 343
York
YO19 5YB
Tel: 01904 466516
www.yorkcourses.co.uk

ALSO AVAILABLE:
An accompanying
COURSE BOOKLET and
TRANSCRIPT of this CD.
Other courses available.

GLIMPSES OF GOD

HOPE FOR TODAY'S
WORLD

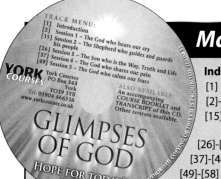

TRACK MENU:
[1] Introduction
[2] Session 1 – The God who hears our cry
[15] Session 2 – The Shepherd who guides and guards his people
[26] Session 3 – The Son who is the Way, Truth and Life
[37] Session 4 – The God who shares our pain
[49] Session 5 – The God who calms our fears

YORK COURSES
PO Box 343
York
YO19 5YB
Tel: 01904 466516
www.yorkcourses.co.uk

ALSO AVAILABLE:
An accompanying
COURSE BOOKLET and
TRANSCRIPT of this CD.
Other courses available.

GLIMPSES OF GOD
HOPE FOR TODAY'S WORLD

Making full use of the CD

Index of Track Numbers

[1]	Introduction
[2]-[14]	Session 1 – The God who hears our cry
[15]-[25]	Session 2 – The Shepherd who guides and guards his people
[26]-[36]	Session 3 – The Son who is the Way, Truth and Life
[37]-[48]	Session 4 – The God who shares our pain
[49]-[58]	Session 5 – The God who calms our fears

Each track number on the course CD corresponds to the start of each new question posed to the participants by Simon Stanley, the presenter. The track numbers are shown in square brackets in the text of the transcript itself.

When to play the CD/audiotape

There is no 'right' way! Some groups will play the 14-minute piece at the beginning of the session. Other groups do things differently – perhaps playing it at the end, or playing 7/8 minutes at the beginning and the rest halfway through the meeting. The track markers (on the CD and shown in the Transcript) will help you find any question put to the participants very easily, including the Closing Reflections, which you may wish to play (again) at the end of the session. Do whatever is best for you and your group.

COPYRIGHT:

The image as used on the course booklet, CD and the front cover of this booklet is copyright at dreamstime.com

Photo of Canon David Winter by kind permission of the Church Times

Full details of our range, including the latest special offers and discounts, are available at www.yorkcourses.co.uk where you can order securely online.

FREE PACKING & SECOND CLASS POST IN THE UK

SUBSIDISED OVERSEAS POSTAGE

USING THE AUDIOTAPE

The *Introduction* and *Sessions* 1 and 2 are on Side A. *Sessions* 3, 4 and 5 are on Side B.

This transcript accompanies the course booklet for *GLIMPSES OF GOD – Hope for today's world*

YORK COURSES

A COURSE IN FIVE SESSIONS WRITTEN BY DAVID WINTER
ACCOMPANYING CD/AUDIOTAPE AND TRANSCRIPT AVAILABLE

GLIMPSES OF GOD

HOPE FOR TODAY'S WORLD

York Courses presents

GLIMPSES OF GOD -
Hope for today's world

Welcome to York Courses *and* Glimpses of God – Hope for today's world. *I'm Simon Stanley and I'm delighted to welcome former Archbishop of York, Dr David Hope, to introduce the course and to tell you something about our contributors. David Hope.*

DH: Another year, another Lent Course – and I'm delighted to be able to introduce this one with just as much enthusiasm as I have its predecessors.

Glimpses of God is a most timely course, which looks for evidence of God's presence and activity in a world beset by so many moral conundrums.

Canon David Winter, a prolific author and broadcaster and one-time Head of Religious Broadcasting at the BBC, makes a strong case in the course booklet for a listening and compassionate God who continues to guard and guide his children, not only calming our fears but also sharing our pain.

Here on the CD some of the issues he raises are discussed, examined and commented upon by this year's contributors, whom it's my pleasure now to introduce to you.

Baroness Williams of Crosby – Shirley Williams – is a British politician, academic and author. Co-founder of the Liberal Democrats, and a member of the House of Lords since 1993, she is also Professor Emeritus of Elective Politics at Harvard University and a member of the International Commission on Nuclear Non Proliferation and Disarmament. She's a Roman Catholic and attends worship regularly, often with her grandson.

Bishop Stephen Cottrell was appointed Bishop of Chelmsford in 2010. Before ordination he worked in the film industry, and for a year at St Christopher's Hospice in Sydenham. A member of the Governing Body of the College of Evangelists, he is the author of numerous books, including the text for the acclaimed York Course *Rich Inheritance – Jesus' legacy of love.*

The return to a York Course by the Reverend Professor Dr David Wilkinson is very welcome. A Methodist minister and Principal of St John's College, University of Durham, David has doctorates in astrophysics and theology. He's an author and regular contributor to Radio 2's *Pause for Thought* and Radio 4's *Thought for the Day.*

The Revd Lucy Winkett is the Rector of St James Piccadilly. Previously she was Precentor at St Paul's Cathedral in London. She was the author of Archbishop Rowan Williams' Lent Book *Our Sound is Our Wound* and writes and broadcasts on themes of culture, religion, music and gender. She's also a regular contributor to Radio 4's *Thought for the Day*.

So there we are. Once again, I wish you every blessing as you meet to consider such important issues. They are actually important issues not just for the Church, but for the whole world. If by thinking, talking, sharing views and, yes, praying your way through *Glimpses of God* you find a little more confidence in engaging with others outside the church community, who are also seeking answers to these big questions – then this course will have achieved what it sets out to do.

1

Glimpses of God
Session 1:

THE GOD WHO HEARS OUR CRY

Hello, I'm Simon Stanley and I'll be guiding you through this course as our contributors – Bishop Stephen Cottrell, Baroness Shirley Williams and Professor David Wilkinson – explore how we might recognise the presence of God in today's world and discover hope for our own times. So how can we believe in a God of love, when we're assailed by disasters and wars and illness? Where is the evidence that God even hears our cry in the midst of our suffering? I asked each of our contributors what personal experience they had of suffering, and none had experienced it themselves, but they were all challenged by contact with those who had – and it had life-changing effects on them. David Wilkinson finds the challenge of suffering a spur to remould his faith.

DW: I think the times when I've really struggled with faith have been seeing loved ones go through the mill. Either illnesses to children, or illnesses to my wife, or illnesses to parents, because as you go through struggle you sense, is God loving? Is he there? And as a scientist I want to always say yeah, there's going to be negative evidence and positive evidence. So the reminder of what God has done in the past. And then a remoulding of faith. I actually think faith is a living thing. It develops; it changes. There's nothing wrong in that, and suffering has often brought that about.

[3] *When the young Stephen Cottrell felt called to become a priest, he was challenged by a wise, older friend to test* out his vocation by going to work at a hospice. He went. And it changed him.

SC: I worked there for the best part of a year as a ward orderly, living and working with the dying. And I didn't get an answer to the question of 'why does God allow suffering?' But it did change the way I approached the question, because from that experience I no longer say to myself, 'where is God in the suffering?' rather I ask the question, 'how can *I* be the hands, the heart, the eyes, the love of Christ when I encounter suffering?'

[4] *Shirley Williams has lost many family members, often after long and painful illness. She couldn't answer why, any more than the others, but she did find enormous power in praying for them when they were ill.*

SW: I think prayer's effective in a way that's strange. That's to say that I think when the person who is at risk knows that many people are praying for him or her, I've noticed its amazing power that comes to them the – as it were – the desire to keep fighting if they're ill, the desire to die peacefully if they're elderly and have reached the point in life where they're likely to die. I think prayer is – it has a kind of mysterious way of extra-ordinarily reaching the person you pray for. And that's terribly important. I don't think it's so much asking for a miracle – though I have done that once or twice – I think it's recognising that you are identifying with a person who's suffering, or who's just died. And that identification somehow, in a curious way, reaches them.

[5] *So what about prayer? If it doesn't work directly, what's the point? Stephen points out that we are part of the answer to prayer.*

SC: You should dare not utter a prayer if you are not yourself prepared to be the answer to that prayer. You know – prayer is a dangerous business. It's not about us trying to change God's mind. On the contrary, it's about placing ourselves in that right relationship with God where we invite God to change *our* minds, where we invite God to use us to be the answer to our *own* prayers, so that the cry of *our* heart resonates with the cry of God's heart.

[6] *And David finds answers to prayer come in different ways at different times.*

DW: Sometimes I've prayed and God has answered in a miraculous type of way, where I never expected something to happen, and things have just fallen into place without me having to do anything. Sometimes I've asked for things in prayer where the answer has been quite clearly, no. And then there are other moments in prayer where God has said: part of discipleship is learning about partnership on the journey. The kingdom that Jesus introduced was, of course, focused primarily in Jesus' power and presence. But in calling disciples, what he does is he shares the responsibility. And it's that sense of receiving responsibility in prayer that's very profound.

[7] *St Paul tells us in the letter to the Romans, that all things work together, for good, for those who love God. But do they really? Stephen Cottrell.*

SC: That isn't my everyday experience. But at the same time I've had so many other experiences where something, which seemed futile, useless, senseless to me, has been turned around by God and used for his purposes. And so I suppose it's wise for us to remember that God is a redeemer – that, therefore, whatever we do – however much we mess it up – God will not throw that away. Rather he will take it, redeem it, use it to his glory.

[8] *David sets 'all things working for good' in its wider, scriptural context.*

DW: When Paul in Romans 8 talks about all things working for good, that comes at the end of eight chapters of discussion about God as the creator – the one who redeems us, who's shown his love to us in Jesus, who's worked through and beyond and overcome the consequences of our sin, who's given the Holy Spirit. And yet at the same time there's a sense of the 'not-yet-ness' about God's purposes being fulfilled. And so, you get this image of the whole creation groaning – looking forward to that which is to come. Then Paul says: now in the understanding of that big story, know that these things are working out for good. I don't think he means that every small detail is being pushed by God – the type of theology which says, 'oh, this happened for a purpose'. And so I think often there are aspects which I'm very hesitant to say, 'well, God sent that for this purpose'. I want to be a little more cautious and so let's wait until we see the big picture and then I think, I hope, I trust, I believe that there we see a God who's working for a new creation.

[9] *Of course, a great deal of suffering is caused by exploitation and injustice. I asked Stephen if Christians are ever justified in using force to oppose evil.*

SC: I take the position that Christians should only use force in very, very limited and certain circumstances, where the use of limited and proportionate force may – or we believe will – prevent an even greater hurt or harm or catastrophe. Therefore that follows into what the Church often refers to as the 'just war' theory. Which I do believe in, when applied critically and carefully.

[10] *So, what exactly is the 'just war' theory? Shirley Williams.*

SW: The concept of the 'just war' is actually, I think, a very wise concept. I mean it basically says that first of all that war must always be proportionate; it says that war must always be the last resort; it says that war must, as far as it conceivably can, avoid the – injury to civilians. But it's – in saying that you don't rule out war completely, but that war has to be justified, both when it's going on and in starting it, I think frankly it would have stopped quite a lot of wars in our time. I would think that there would not have been a war in Iraq, if people had taken the views of 'just war' absolutely seriously. The cause was, as it later turned out, muddled and unclear. I think it would have raised large questions about the war in Afghanistan as well. I think the 'just war' concept is one that would probably have applied to the Second World War – because of the particularly evil nature of the Nazi regime – but I doubt that it would have applied for the First World War, which was essentially a war for territory.

[11] *We're so aware through the media of needs across the world, that it's not surprising we speak about 'compassion fatigue'. I asked Shirley how we can overcome it and still do something to help.*

SW: I think, probably, the way round that fatigue is to personalise it. To get, for example, things like 'Adopt a Grandmother'. I've got an adopted grandmother in India somewhere – not that I've ever met her. But the fact she is described as a grandmother, the fact I get letters about her, gives me some personal sense of my link to that family. And as the world goes global, what's rather encouraging is that that is beginning to become stronger. And that's why I think the idea of linking up rich countries, rich communities, rich families with poor communities in poor countries is a terribly important part of showing compassion nowadays.

[12] *In the booklet, David Winter says that some suffering arises from 'living on an unpredictable planet in a purposefully random universe'. I asked Stephen if the phrase resonated with him.*

SC: Yes, I found that a provocatively helpful phrase, because I think what lies behind it is the understanding that we live in a universe that God has created, as it were, to create itself. That part of the DNA of the universe is that creativity – which is itself the hallmark and the thumbprint of the creator God. So this universe which is also creating itself – subject to the laws of the universe, which we are beginning to learn more and more about – what they tell us is about the incredible fragile equilibrium of our current planet. You know, just a couple of degrees one way or a couple of degrees the other way, and there wouldn't be life at all as we know it. And yet what that also brings with it are volcanoes and earthquakes and the shifting of tectonic plates and all the other stuff that goes with that. And therefore part of living as we are within this universe means that we will be living with the consequences of that.

Which is both human life as we know it, in all its abundant joy, but also the presence of tornadoes and hurricanes and droughts and floods – terrible things which God has not *sent*, to *test* us or *punish* us, but are part of the way the universe must be, if we are to be. Now that's a hard thing for us to accept – especially if you're living in the path of a tsunami – and so, I don't say that in any way as an answer to the problems of the world. But I do think acknowledging and understanding that that's the way the universe is, and that we have to live with it, is quite a helpful way of thinking about it.

[13] *David looked at it as a scientist. The old idea of Newton that the world works like a clock and is totally predictable just won't do any more.*

DW: We now know that the world is much more subtle, much more interesting, much more complex. It has something called 'quantum theory' as part of it, which at the very basis of matter has an uncertainty to it. It has something called 'chaos' in it. And chaos – well, the best description of chaos is why we can't predict whether it will rain in Manchester in three weeks' time. However much data you have, and however big a computer you have, you just cannot predict completely. There's an openness to the future within the physical process. Now that makes the whole discussion very complex, but – I think it guards us from some of the kind of theology which says, 'well, everything's determined' or 'God simply pokes his finger in and pushes that'. That's a very naïve view of the world – both scientifically and biblically, it seems to me.

[14] *And now Lucy Winkett reflects on the God who hears our cry.*

The theologian Gustavo Guttiérez said that the most important thing about what Jesus said while he was on the cross was not *what* he said, but the fact that he said anything at all. Jesus, the subject of torture, cruelty and inhumane violence, by crying out on the cross taught human beings to do the same. We are shown by this example not to remain silent in the face of injustice and suffering: to cry out even in desolation that we think God has abandoned us. It's our calling to speak, to cry, to shout when we experience or witness the inhumanity that is a hallmark of life in the world. Every news report brings a different litany of national disasters and conflicts, but the suffering, the hollowing out of hearts by grief, continues. Composers of music have often set these seven last words of Jesus, sometimes using the words themselves and sometimes writing instrumental music as a meditation. Haydn's *Seven Last Words* is a piece written for string quartet and the power of the wordless music expresses in a beautiful way the ugliness of the cross. The beauty is not an anaesthetic however; the twentieth-century mystic Simone Weil wrote that beauty is like 'small tears in the surface of the world that pull us through to a vaster space'. God hears our cry in wordless beauty or chanted slogan, and these truthful cries are 'tears in the surface of the world'. In crying out, we pray that we will be drawn beyond what we have thought of, deeper into a vaster and more intimate communion between suffering humanity and a suffering God.

Glimpses of God
Session 2: CD Track [15]

THE SHEPHERD WHO GUARDS AND GUIDES HIS PEOPLE

The notion of the Good Shepherd is a key theme in both Hebrew and Christian Scriptures. But is it still applicable today? Shirley Williams thinks it is – but more specifically in reference to Jesus.

SW: Most Christians think about the Good Shepherd in terms of Jesus rather than of God. Because God is such a huge concept to try and get one's mind around that the shepherd image conflicts to some extent. I mean, the way I tend to see God is more in terms of Matthew Arnold – 'the forces of the sea, the forces of the sky; the stars in the sky' and so forth. It's the universal that is the closest I get to having some sense of what God is – and his omnipotence and so forth. I think in the case of Christ he is, he personalises, he humanises the concept of God. And therefore the idea of the Good Shepherd, which is obviously more appropriate to scriptural times than to now – but nevertheless echoes now – is something most of us associate with Jesus Christ.

[16] *Part of the imagery of shepherding is of guiding and of protecting. I asked David Wilkinson whether he could give an example of God's guidance, and he said that whilst he felt clearly guided as a young man, as he got older he felt much less certain about it. It worried him until he realised why that is.*

DW: As we grow older God wants us to take more responsibility. Just as a parent, there's a certain level of guidance that I give to my children when they're two or four year old, to what I give them now when they're eighteen and sixteen, as we grow in Christian faith there are moments where God actually says to us: 'what do *you* think? What do *you* want to do? You know my will, you know what I'm about, you know what it means to be a disciple. There may be a number of options – now learn through taking responsibility.' And I found that a very helpful way of understanding how God may guide as you grow as a Christian.

[17] *What about feeling protected by the Good Shepherd? Stephen Cottrell cites the Old Testament story of Shadrach, Meshach and Abednego being thrown by King Nebuchadnezzar into the fiery furnace, for not worshipping a golden idol. And the story goes they weren't burnt. But it's not their survival that impresses Stephen – rather, it's their attitude before they're thrown in.*

SC: *Before* they're thrown into the fire they say to King Nebuchadnezzar, 'whether our God saves us or not, we're not going to bow down and worship this great statue you've made.' Now it's *that* attitude which I think is the really godly, Christian one. That we say to the world, 'well, whether I suffer or not – and I know I will, we're all going to suffer, we're all going to die – but whatever happens to me, I'm going to be true to my Christian faith and to my Christian principles. God may save me in the way that I hope he might, or he may not. But that isn't going to change the fact that I'm going to carry on believing and behaving in this way.'

[18] *Still in the Old Testament, the best known Shepherd passage is Psalm 23* The Lord's my Shepherd, *which contains the famous verse, 'though I walk through the valley of the shadow of death I will fear no*

evil'. I asked David what he could say that might help those who are right there now.

DW: In the very honest way of trying to help people we say some really silly things. I remember a friend of mine saying that, when he was a small boy, his sister was killed in a road accident. And at the funeral service the vicar, well meaning – dealing with the death of a child – said, 'God wanted another star in heaven.' At that point my friend, as a seven year-old, said, 'what rubbish! First of all, that's not what stars are about anyway. And second, that doesn't do any justice to the person who was drunk-driving, who killed my sister.' Now, I think theology, and thinking through these issues, often tells us what not to say in the shadow of the valley of death, rather than what *to* say. It cautions us about giving easy answers. And it reminds us that sometimes we just have to live with uncertainty, and without a neat and easy picture to reply.

[19] *It was quite popular some years ago to try to rewrite the 23rd Psalm into current images: 'The Lord is my Social Worker' and so on – to make it somehow more relevant. But Stephen thinks that the sheep/shepherd image still works well, if we understand its history and context properly.*

SW: The biblical shepherds led from the front themselves. Lived *with* the sheep, you know that's – lived out in the mountains with the sheep. It was a dangerous, wild kind of existence. The shepherd often *was* the gate to the sheepfold, you know – literally protecting them. There's a wonderful example in the David narratives, where, you know, the young shepherd boy, David, is questioned about whether he's the right man to go out and slay Goliath.

Well, David puffs himself up and in his defence says, 'I'm a shepherd! If a lion comes into the fold I kill it! And I'm jolly well going to go and kill this giant, Goliath!' So yes, 'shepherd' in the Bible is very different from 'shepherd' in our imaginations today. So should we get rid of the shepherd language? I'm not so sure.

[20] *David does think there is need to represent biblical material for our own time.*

DW: For me, part of the challenge for the Church is, begin to think about how we translate the Scriptures into the indigenous language of city-dwellers; what it means for me to talk about the guidance and providence of God within the area of science, where people want to ask questions – not of the sheep and the shepherd, but of quantum theory and chaos, and how does God actually relate to the science of the world.

[21] *The last words of Jesus, the Good Shepherd, in Matthew's Gospel are: 'Lo, I am with you always.' I asked David and Stephen to reflect on this promise.*

DW: Looking back on a few decades now of being a Christian, there are moments where I've sensed the presence of God – but not until very much later seen the workings of God. And there have been times when I've looked back, even without a sense of the presence of God, and seen the power of God at work. It's often only with hindsight that I see that.

SC: I do believe Jesus is with me always. But I don't always – it doesn't always feel like that. And I shouldn't simply rely on my feelings, which are always going to let me down, or be subject to my mood and other things. Rather, I must look to those virtuous habits, those spiritual disciplines which will not only sustain me, but nurture in me that sense that God is with me. And so I kind of say to myself, 'if each day I can hear God speaking to me in scripture; if each day I can speak with God in prayer and listen to his word for me; if each day I can behold God in a broken piece of bread – well, then I might start seeing him all over the place and know him in all kinds of unexpected people. And then I'll know that he's with me always.'

[22] *The Bible passages we've been considering were once part of the nation's consciousness – commonplace ideas. But this can hardly be said to be true today. Is Britain still a Christian country in any real meaning of the word? Shirley Williams.*

SW: Not really. When I look back at the institutional presence of Christianity – if I go back to my grandparents – the knowledge of Christianity, the constant presence of the Scriptures, the going to Church to hear them – a great deal of that has gone. And I think there's a kind of fuzzy, warm, teddy bear-like feeling about Christianity in a lot of quarters. But that's not really what it is to be Christian. So I suppose I have to say we're a post-Christian society. So I think that those of us who are Christians have got an awful lot of work to do. Now what in a way, for me, is the centre of Christianity is the lessons and teachings of Jesus Christ – the New Testament. And I think it's an amazing document. And I think it is, almost certainly, the way that we should learn to live. But it has to be said that the institutional Churches have not really been quite the messengers of Christianity – and particularly of Christ's teaching – that they ought to be. And for me, absolutely

central is something which is very hard for those of us, including the Churches, who are involved with power relationships, to understand at all, which is the nature of the victory of the cross. Because the victory of the cross is not a victory of power. It's a victory of anti-power. And the fact that Christianity is built around the victory of sacrifice is *terribly* important, but it's something I think that the institutional Churches, over centuries, tended to forget. They got tempted by power. They misused, as well as using power, and they came, to some extent, away from the teachings of Christ.

[23] *For Stephen Cottrell it's yes and no.*

SC: Christianity has obviously and manifestly shaped our laws, our culture, our way of life. So yes, in terms of the heritage, in terms of the way we still often think about ourselves, yes, Britain is still a Christian country. But if we mean are we people who are motivated by the joys and demands of the Christian faith, I think the answer must be, no we're not. In many ways our way of life is very distant from the Christian way, and I think getting more distant.

[24] *David Wilkinson reports that a few years ago at St John's College, Durham, they undertook the first national survey on biblical literacy, interviewing 1,000 people. They discovered a massive ignorance about what is in the Bible.*

DW: For example, we asked people what they knew about the parable of the Good Samaritan and found that over 60% of people actually knew nothing about the parable of the Good Samaritan – I mean *literally* nothing. But the other interesting thing that came out of the survey, and wasn't picked up as much by the media, was the hunger for biblical teaching and biblical knowledge. And I think what we are in is in a situation where our nation has become post-Christian. Well, we're not too far away from the world of the New Testament. And some of the principles of the New Testament might help us again in refocusing mission, and finding a real joy in what it means to witness, perhaps to people for the first time, of what the Good News of Jesus is all about.

[25] *And now we turn to Lucy Winkett for her reflection.*

Just outside the town of Bethlehem in the West Bank is an area called Beit Sahour. It's the place where tradition has it the shepherds saw the angels announcing the birth of Jesus. When I stood there not long ago, taking in the modern detritus of rubbish and rubble – what in Britain would be called a brownfield site – I held my breath, as a real shepherd with a small flock of sheep appeared from a nearby field and crossed the road to the patch of ground on which I was standing. I was transfixed by seeing a Palestinian shepherd, even though the walls with barbed wire, the check points and the rapidly expanding Security Barrier cutting off Bethlehem from its surroundings made imagining first-century Palestine impossible. This was a shepherd on the outskirts of town; a living rural icon approaching a modern city and encountering the blue plastic bottles, the brown paper bags and piles of stones that seem to characterise urban waste across the world. The shepherd was leaning on a crook, just as you might expect, and the few sheep, not particularly well fed, were scavenging what they could from the

stony ground. A tank rolled past. They hardly looked up. When Jesus of Nazareth said he was the Good Shepherd, he was describing himself in a peaceful role in a similarly militarised society, a familiar sight to his audience.

Most of us need help with this image. Shepherds and sheep belong to a stable agrarian society, not a twenty-first-century city; but imagining God as a shepherd is to realise that God is in the midst of us, walking ahead and beside us, urging us on. Searching for us. Jesus the Good Shepherd is a picture of God who is our friend; who knows us by name, whose voice we recognise, in whose arms we are safe, and on whose shoulders we are set and taken home. And just like the Palestinian shepherd in Beit Sahour, Jesus Christ approaches our modern violent cities with a message of presence and peace: 'I am'. Good news for lost people.

If you are listening to the audiotape, please fast-forward it to the end of Side A at this point. Session 3 starts at the beginning of Side B.

Glimpses of God
Session 3: CD Track [26]

THE SON WHO IS THE WAY, TRUTH AND LIFE

In the course booklet, David Winter writes about 'the God who makes himself known to us'. I asked our contributors to tell us a story or two to illustrate their own journey of faith. Shirley Williams, Stephen Cottrell and David Wilkinson, in that order.

SW: A particular moment that I remember, when I was rather foolishly climbing over the Cuillins in Skye. I'd started, for some mad reason, after lunch. And by the time I got to the top of the Cuillins it was already – the sun was setting. And the Cuillins are pretty savage mountains, scary mountains. And in the sort of dusk I climbed up what later turned out to be a pinnacle. And suddenly realising I was completely stuck – I couldn't see a way up – well, the way up was nowhere. And I couldn't see a way down. And literally, in the last ray of the setting sun, a streak of light showed me the way down. And I was able to piece my way from one, literally, foothold to another – 'cause this was completely vertical – hanging on with my fingers and my toes. And got down to the Saddle again. And I've always thought that this was a sort of divine moment. I did pray – and it was an extraordinary moment of answered prayer of a very striking kind.

SC: When I was ordained as a deacon in my mid-twenties, my Auntie Millie came to the ordination service. Now, Auntie Millie was my grandma's best friend. And my Auntie Millie was a devout Roman Catholic – the sort of devout Roman Catholic that pretty much went to Mass every day of her life. And at the party afterwards (this is what she told me) she told me that every day for the last – I don't know, forty years – she had prayed for the conversion of my family when she went to Mass. Because, you know, her – my grandma, her best friends, you know, none of us really were, you know, were people of faith. Pretty much a pagan lot. And she'd made that her intention, when she went to Mass every day, to pray for our conversion. Now, if you'd have spoken to me the day *before* I was ordained as a deacon, and said to me, 'so, Stephen, tell me about your Christian journey', I would have told you this long complicated story which was all about decisions I had made. And then suddenly I find out, that even before I was born, there was somebody, every day, praying that my family would come to faith in Jesus Christ. And suddenly, my whole understanding of my own story was changed. Now I don't understand how that works. I don't understand all of that. But I do believe that one of the reasons I'm sitting here now, speaking to you, is because of my Auntie Millie's prayers.

DW: I became a Christian at the age of seventeen and – for three main reasons. The first was that I fell desperately in love with a girl in the local Christian youth group and so started to go along to this church to try and get a date with her. Didn't get a date with her ever! But found that amongst these Christian young people was something that I didn't have – some kind of experience in life which I hadn't come across before. Second reason was that Bob Dylan went through his Christian phase. I was a great fan of Bob Dylan and suddenly I heard songs about Jesus in *my* culture, in *my* language, rather than the language of the eighteenth century. That was very profound for me, and has stayed with me. And the third reason was that I started to read the New Testament. Here, I just became fascinated with the story of the man Jesus.

[27] *Jesus' famous claim in John 14 that, 'I am the way, the truth and the life. No one comes to the Father but by me' can sound exclusive. Does it mean that non-Christians are to be excluded from God's presence? Stephen Cottrell answers by taking a look at the stories Jesus told.*

SC: The hero of some of his best-known stories are all people of other faiths or other cultures: a good Samaritan, a Syrophoenician woman, a Samaritan woman at the well. So we need to be very, very careful about taking to ourselves that which belongs to God i.e. the judgement of others. So, just as Jesus was a 'good Jew', and all his first followers were 'good Jews', I believe that wherever we see goodness in people of other faiths – or of no faith at all – we should honour and respect and delight in that. And I certainly don't believe it's my place – or anyone's place – to sit in judgement on those of other faiths.

[28] *Shirley Williams welcomes more openness between denominations and faiths.*

SW: One of the things that *is* good about the modern world is that we are much less denominational and bigoted than we used to be. It is important that the Pope and the Archbishop and the Chief Rabbi can stand on a religious ceremony together. It is important in this country, which wouldn't have dreamt of it, if you go back to the early beginning of the last century. That's very good. I think it's a recognition that the paths to God are many.

[29] *David Wilkinson wants to be open too, but is keen not to lose the centrality of Christ.*

DW: Although I want to be very clear to say I believe that all salvation is through Jesus – that he is the way, the truth and the life – I want to be very cautious then about saying who's in and who's out. I find amongst my friends who are Muslims or Jewish – those following the Abrahamic faiths – a real sense at the heart that salvation is through the mercy and grace of God, rather than simply by our own works. And therefore I think God respects and honours that. As long as, for *me* the understanding is, that the mechanism for salvation is through Christ.

[30] *For Christians, Jesus is Lord, our great leader. I wondered what qualities our contributors look for in leaders. Shirley has been a political leader for many years.*

SW: The very first quality is recognising that leadership is service and not imposition. I suppose one goes back again to something like Mandela, Gorbachev and so forth. There are quite a lot of examples of amazingly humble leaders. There are a great many examples of tremendously self-important leaders and mostly they go awry – quite quickly, I think. But it's not easy to be a humble leader. It means that you're much more open to the slings and arrows of criticism than somebody who is more self-confident – more sure that he's right. And it also means that you are learning all the time and not just teaching what you once learnt. That's the first quality. The second quality, I think, is moral courage. When it comes to the big moral issues – whether it's in a company because it's, let's say, corrupt. Or whether it's in politics, where the temptation is always to be populist – over things like capital punishment, and so on. Or whether it's global, where again the temptation is to strut around the place boasting military power, what's quite clear is that the number of men and women with moral courage is a limited number. They're not all leaders. Some of them are individually, colossally morally courageous, which I do think is quite a rare quality.

[31] *What does Stephen, as a Church leader, think is essential to his position?*

SC: When I first became the Bishop of Chelmsford, people kept on saying to me, 'oh, Bishop, what's your vision?' And I always replied by saying, 'I haven't got one'. Which came as a bit of a surprise, 'cause I think people think: oh well, one thing we know about leaders is they're supposed to have a vision. And I thought: well, why pretend you've got one if you haven't. But the other thing is, I simply don't see Christian leadership in that way that, you know – who cares what *my* vision is for the Church? What matters is *God's* vision. And I don't believe in that kind of heroic knight-on-a-white-charger model of leadership, where one person is uniquely placed to receive the vision from God. Rather, I believe God's vision is communicated to God's Church, and *together* we seek the mind of Christ for his Church in his world. So the first thing I look for in a Christian leader is someone who is themselves prepared to be led. Somebody who will be *seeking* the mind of Christ for the Church.

[32] *David spends his life training people to become Christian leaders.*

DW: The model for leadership for me, which I would love to emulate, and indeed try and aspire to, is of course the model of Jesus himself. Of someone who blends self-understanding with humility. Who blends an openness to working with others with a sense of clear purpose and leadership. And someone who blends deep humanity with intimacy with God.

[33] *Holman Hunt's famous picture* The Light of the World *suggests that Jesus can only enter our lives if we open the door and let him in – a personal relationship with Jesus. I wondered if Stephen feels that he knows Jesus personally.*

SC: Yes, I do know Jesus personally. Where and how do I know him? Through scripture, through prayer, through the sacramental life – and, supremely, in other people. So I, I live out that personal relationship with Jesus by trying to see the face of Christ in everyone I meet, and in every encounter that I have. Now, don't misunderstand me, I'm well aware how far I fall short of that in what actually happens in my life. But it's what I expect. So it's not my personal thing with Jesus which helps me to survive a difficult, dark and troublesome world. On the contrary, it is *within* the delights and challenges of the world that I will encounter Jesus in the people that I meet in my daily life. So that's what *I* mean by a personal relationship with Jesus.

[34] *David thinks we have to be careful in our use of intimate language, which can lead to a partial view of the place of Christ in our lives.*

DW: The model that we have in the New Testament of God becoming a human being I think gives us some basis on which, as long as we're aware of its limitations, we can use this type of language. The difficulty is where we reduce God to those images. Where we make God completely in our own image. And so, you know, Jesus becomes my mate – and that's all he is. Whereas, in fact, not only is he friend, he's also Lord.

[35] *Just a final question about the Bible, which is full of sublime teaching like the Sermon on the Mount, and also some pretty awful violence and apparent hatred. Can we pick and choose? How are we to understand how scripture works? Stephen makes his point by looking at the Sermon on the Mount.*

SC: In the Sermon on the Mount Jesus himself is quoting the Old Testament. And he says things like, 'you've heard it said' but what he means is, 'you've read about it in the Old Testament', so 'you've heard it said: an eye for an eye and a tooth for a tooth, but I tell you if someone hits you on one cheek, offer him the other. You've heard it said you must love your friend and hate your enemy, but *I* say to you …' So in other words, Jesus himself acknowledges that within the whole narrative of scripture there are things which we are now called upon to reinterpret, in the light of God's revelation of himself in Jesus Christ.

[36] *And so Lucy takes us back to our title for this session – I am the Way, the Truth and the Life:*

If ever there was a top ten chart of misused scriptural verses then this phrase has to be one of the hits. The description of Christ as 'the Way, the Truth and the Life' has sometimes been used as what one theologian calls a 'clobber text': a way of drawing a line between 'us' who are right and 'them' who are wrong – within Christianity itself and between Christianity and other world faiths. Jesus' phrase recorded by John is a beautiful and poetic way of describing human life lived to its fullest creative potential. If we concentrate only on the 'way', then life of faith becomes just a matter of ethical actions. If we concentrate only on 'truth' then we become focused on dogma to the exclusion of other perspectives. The third quality, 'life', is the one which together with ethics and belief, can make discipleship vibrant, imaginative, full of promise and hope, and grounded in love. What's being offered to us as friends and followers of Christ is no more and no less than a life. Whenever you hear yourself saying or thinking: 'what shall I do with my life?' – see how you're spending your hours and days. That's what you're doing with your life. We're already doing it; real life is now with the people God has given us to love; our time is here to live – and ultimately to give away.

Glimpses of God
Session 4: CD Track [37]

THE GOD WHO SHARES OUR PAIN

Gethsemane was a place of decision and indecision, of courage and of fear. I guessed that our contributors had all had times like that – when they were stretched and painfully challenged. How did they cope? Shirley Williams has been a political fighter all her life, and she carries the scars.

SW: I'm not unused to living through very tough political periods. Luckily, in this country you don't expect to be killed for that! But you'd certainly expect to have a very nasty time, with losing friends, and being abused, and having vast numbers of people writing to you saying that you're a traitor – or whatever you are. I'm quite used to that, and I think that essentially, yes, one does turn to the belief that this is the right thing to do – 'cause that's the only thing that you can hold on to. And that does involve, I think, quite a lot of, sort of, prayerful meditation – hoping that somewhere Christ will recognise what you're up against. You have to really be very careful about it 'cause it's too easy to say: 'this is the right thing to do, so I'm going to do it.' You have to ask yourself at length whether it *is* the right thing to do. Otherwise you just find yourself imposing your political theories on other people, whether they like it or whether they don't. And that's not quite right.

[38] *As a scientist, as well as a theologian, David Wilkinson sometimes finds his faith under severe pressure from the power of philosophical arguments for the very existence of God.*

DW: The intellectual arguments of philosophy for the existence or non-existence of God can cause us quite a lot of heartache and pain at times. And misunderstanding. And they're important. They have to be thought through. But ultimately my faith rests on this man Jesus. God becoming a human being. And it's realising that the Christian faith isn't built on just one thing – that if it snaps, the whole thing collapses. That it's been about being immersed in a story, a narrative, which flows out of the life of Jesus – that's very important.

[39] *Stephen is challenged by Jesus' Gethsemane prayer: 'Not my will, but yours be done'.*

SC: You know in Luke's Gospel he says, 'Father, not my will be done, but yours' and an angel comes to comfort him. But, not much comfort, you know – it says after the angel has left, 'his sweat fell like great drops of blood'. So actually, wasn't it the same for Jesus? He honestly prayed the prayer, but did he have that great inner warmth and comfort that all was well? Well, I don't think he did actually. So perhaps I shouldn't be surprised that I don't either.

[40] *So we can't guarantee an easy ride in our Christian faith. It can be exhausting, as it was for Jesus in Gethsemane – though it was his disciples who actually went to sleep! Shirley understands this well, as far as prayer is concerned.*

SW: The truth of the matter is I'm much more often like the disciples who fall asleep. Because when you get home after a really exhausting day, you have to really force yourself to say a few prayers before you go to bed. Because, in my case often you may have had a, sort of twelve-, fourteen-hour day – and when you get back all you want to do is sleep. Especially if you know you're going to have to get up early in the morning. So it's quite tough to actually force yourself to pray, and very often you fall asleep while you're praying. So in many ways I think that probably for very busy people, prayer associated with a few moments of leisure that one has – or at least of not being perpetually involved in the pressure of work – is a very satisfactory way to pray. Whereas forcing it into the pressures of work isn't always quite such a good idea. So I suppose I might describe myself as an 'unmethodical pray-er' rather a 'methodical pray-er'. There's quite a lot to be said for the discipline of attending church – I do go to church pretty well every week. But I think there's also a lot to be said for the mild serendipity of praying in a situation which elicits prayer – which elicits worship, if you like.

[41] *I wondered how Stephen gets on with prayer.*

SC: I often find prayer hard, combative, boring. I *best* describe myself in prayer as an 'experienced beginner'. You know you hear about these people who are very good at giving up smoking – you know, they've given up thirty times, but they always go back to it six months later. Well, that's me and the spiritual life. I've *started* in the spiritual life many, many times, not got very far and had to reset the compass and start again. So I *feel* like a beginner. But it doesn't change the fact that I think it's the most important thing I do each day. And my prayer is sustained by what I call the disciplines and virtuous habits of the Christian life. And I hang onto them. So the Psalms, the Scriptures, hopefully

some silence, the Eucharist – these things are absolutely central to my life of prayer.

[42] *This session is about the God who shares our pain: Jesus suffering for us and with us. I asked David and Stephen to help us understand what's going on, on the cross.*

DW: The God that I see suffering on the cross remains the God of Love, whose love forgives those who are crucifying him. Whose love eventually will be triumphant in resurrection. Now that is the thing that sustains me. That's a thing that supports me. That's a thing that inspires me. Not just to live with the question of how suffering and the love of God can go together – but also inspires me to do something about it. Because this is an active God doing something about the sin of the world. And so for me the centrality of the cross within Christian places of worship is not just about *my* salvation, it's also a prophetic word for me to go out of that church and to do something about the suffering in the world. Even if I might not understand why it's there.

SC: It's really important that we remember that at his birth Jesus was given two names. But we forget one of them rather too quickly. He was called Jesus, which means 'God saves', and that is one vital reality about the death and the resurrection of Jesus Christ. It is about God saving the world. But his other name is Emmanuel, which means 'God is with us'. And I kind of think that's the first message of the Christian faith. That the first thing that the birth and the life and the cross and the death of Jesus tells us is that our God is with us. He participates in the joys and the sufferings of the world. He plumbs the depths of what it is to be human.

[43] *Assisted dying is much in the news. I asked our contributors about where they stand on this thorny question. First Shirley.*

SW: I have had both relatives and friends who have gone through desperately painful deaths. And, you know, when you see and know and love people who are that – to whom that happens, it's quite hard to say, 'I can't accept that there should be any form of speeding them up on their way' – especially if they ask particularly to be allowed to die. So I think that what one wants to see is more and more support for things like hospices, which enable people to leave this life in a reasonably reconciled way, rather than geriatric wards, where the story is one of the failure of medicine to keep you artificially alive. But I do have to say I think we have a really serious problem, which is that the capacity of medicine to keep people alive, whether or not they particularly want to be kept alive, is now – raises really serious issues. And I think it's going to feed into the idea of assisted dying, unless we begin to recognise that there's a point at which the person who is very ill would naturally die. And ought to be allowed to naturally die. I'm very much for living wills, and very much against the extraordinary intensity of desperate attempts to keep people alive at any price – including the price of their own happiness.

[44] *Stephen worked in a hospice before he trained to be a vicar and endorses Shirley's admiration for those institutions.*

SC: The nurses come round with the drug trolley. I would then come round with the tea trolley. The chaplain would then come round with the Sacraments. It was a holistic ministry – no one thing more important than the other. The cup of tea was as important as the blessed Sacrament – as important as the drugs. We worked together, and people lived life to the full until they died. I'm also aware in my ministry as a priest that, often in those last days of people's lives, there can be a real experience of the presence of God. So I'm deeply suspicious of any legislation that gives us undue control or power over the end of someone's life.

[45] *And David doesn't want us to forget our Christian hope for eternal life.*

DW: What I don't hear in a lot of the conversation about assisted dying is that sense that death is not the end. I think that's a contribution that the Christian Church can make.

[46] *And briefly, a couple of thoughts on the rights and wrongs of suicide.*

SW: I think it's always wrong. But I also think that doing what we used to do, which was to refuse any sanctity to the suicide, was terribly cruel. Because I think many people commit suicide often in a moment of where life is falling in on them.

DW: I wouldn't want to say that suicide was not right, in terms of it being a sin. I don't think the Church has any right to judge on whether it's right or wrong – it's just part of the way that the mess of human life sometimes leads. But there are opportunities for us as Christians to support folk who are struggling – and particularly those groups who do quite outstanding work with those at the risk of suicide.

[47] *Jesus prayed that the cup of suffering might be taken away – avoided.*

But how can the avoidance of conflict ever get us anywhere? Stephen and then David.

SC: Just as none of us likes being unpopular, none of us willingly seeks conflict. But we have to acknowledge the reality of the forces that rage around our world. Its terrible confusions. Its horrors. And as a follower of Jesus Christ we pitch ourselves into the midst of all that, bearing the cross of Jesus Christ. So, there's no way of avoiding both pain and suffering and conflict in this life. And if you think being a Christian will make you immune from it – well, I'd simply suggest you read the Gospels again. They will tell you a very different story.

DW: Sometimes the ignoring of oppression or injustice on a worldwide scale leads to its growth and its development. It's interesting that Jesus, in Gethsemane, asks the question: 'is there another way? Will this cup of suffering be taken from me?' And I think it's entirely right for us to ask of each other, and of God: 'is there another way?' That's a human emotion, but also a constructive emotion, because it allows you to examine a situation and say: 'well actually, no, this is the only way.' But I think sometimes that road of suffering is the only way to go.

[48] *Our final reflection on the God who shares our pain from Lucy Winkett.*

For all of us, pain is a natural part of life. Sometimes our scars are evident; a woman whose face has been burned in a fire walks around a supermarket, wishing that this searing experience is not so apparent to everyone she meets. She would rather be known as a grandmother or a botanist – but she knows people think of her as 'the lady with the burns'. But for most of us our wounds and scars are hidden. When you divorce – the promises you made, and were made to you, are eroded slowly or snapped suddenly and you're alone, perhaps for the first time. Or in grief, when everyone else's voice seems muffled, and your isolation seems complete, when no one – *no one* – will ever be able to know how lonely this feels. When you're made redundant or the diagnosis you get from the doctor is a shock.

When we're suffering, we may not be at all impressed with a God who can feel pain: so what? God saying in effect, 'I feel your pain' sounds hollow when it's accompanied by inaction. Contemplatives say that when they've lived a life dedicated to prayer, they experience the presence of God as an intense joy and intense pain at the same time; a paradox that is somehow true. As is this: at the very moment when isolation and shame are at their profoundest, that is the very moment that God is with you in the mess. At the very moment when you have no idea what to say, what to pray, even whether you want to have anything to do with such a God; God is not elsewhere. God is here.

Glimpses of God
Session 5:

CD Track [49]

THE GOD WHO CALMS OUR FEARS

'Don't be anxious about tomorrow', says Jesus. But we are. Some worry more than others, of course, as Shirley Williams told me.

SW: My mother was a great worrier. She – when I used to go out on a bike ride, she'd usually think I wouldn't come back – alive. And that was, I think, a direct – direct follow-through from her experience in the First World War where she lost every young man in her family – or every young man she knew. And therefore, to her, you know, the knock on the door was the telegram that said: 'Lieutenant Brittain has died.' And therefore she was a terrible worrier. Worried all the time. And I think partly because of that I just didn't. I've never worried much. I look sympathetically at people who worry, because I think it's an awful burden to carry. But it ain't mine. So, I think I have to answer your question by saying, 'Hardly ever.'

[50] From childhood, Stephen Cottrell has taken the advice of not being anxious seriously.

SC: The authorised version for this text, which is imprinted in my mind – first bit of scripture I ever learnt by heart – was: 'sufficient unto the day is the evil thereof' which the modern translation's far less poetic – a bit easier to understand: 'today has enough trouble of its own, you know, don't worry about tomorrow.' And I think this bit of scripture got inside me, at a very, you know, formative stage of my life. And I

think for my own Christian journey it is absolutely central. That the call of the Christian life is the call to enter joyfully and passionately into the present moment. It is the only thing we possess with any certainty. You know, what's gone has gone. We have to live with the consequences of it, you know – we can't get it back. But what you can be as a Christian is reconciled to it, by seeking the forgiveness, mercy, presence of Jesus Christ. And tomorrow – well, who knows about tomorrow? We don't quite know what's going to happen next. What do we possess with certainty? *Now!* And if I could practise that presence of God in every moment, looking to behold God's presence – well, I *would* be in heaven. That would be heaven on earth – you know, what Jesus calls us to pray for.

[51] David Wilkinson knows he shouldn't worry, but sometimes he does.

DW: I have a very strong sense – and I've always had this from the first point of when I became a Christian – of God's sovereign working out his purposes for good. But I think when things become closer to home, and on certain issues, I do worry. I worry about if those close to me are really struggling. And there, I can be as panicky as anyone else. And that's where sometimes a paralysis in prayer for me comes in. That, if it's really close at home, if it's really close at home – that's where I can struggle. Although not really too much about my own life, I feel quite relaxed about that.

[52] All three of our contributors are in, or have been in, positions of leadership. And leaders are sometimes called upon to make unpopular decisions. I wondered how Stephen and David cope.

18

SC: The way I deal with this, when I know that I have said or done something that I know some people won't like, is I try to ask myself the question: 'where am I getting my affirmation?' Yes, of course it's nice to get affirmation from other people, of course it is. But that's not what it's about. *I am going to be held accountable to God for my leadership in the Church.* And I take that very seriously. And so that's where, you know, if I can stand before God and give an account for the decisions I've made – okay, I'm sure I've got many wrong – but if I can actually say, 'I truly believed this was the right thing to do', you know, I'd rather take my chances there, than court the popularity of the world, only to stand before God and say, 'well, yeah, I knew it wasn't the right thing to do – but it was a great vote winner.'

DW: Sometimes unpopular decisions have to be taken for justice or for long-term good. And that's where I think one has to listen well – not just to the different options, but to the real sense of injustice and pain that unpopular decisions bring. But also one has to be bold and confident in trying to look at the bigger picture, and find resources – for me, within my relationship with God, which says: I'm going to try and trust that this is the best thing to do, even if it may be really unpopular at the time.

[53] *In matters of faith, Jesus says that a tiny amount, as big as a mustard seed, he says, can move mountains. Which is just as well, because among Christians there seems to be a very uneven distribution – from total belief to being plagued with doubt. Where, I wondered, were our contributors on this spectrum? Shirley.*

SW: It's very difficult to be a person of simple faith. I'm not. I think that my faith is much assailed. And you remember St Thomas' famous phrase, you know, 'Lord I believe, help thou my unbelief.' That's exactly where I'm at. Because although I believe to some extent, I'm also very open to doubt, and have to confront it. And I think, given the world of intellectual thought, it's quite hard to avoid that. Maybe it's a lovely position, blessed position, not to be like that. But I think most of us in a modern, relatively – little 'l' liberal – society tend to be assailed by doubt. But it's not just doubt about God, it's also doubt about almost everything else, almost everything we do, almost every relationship – we're taught to question it. Perhaps more than we should be. And so, religion is religion in the face of doubt, rather than religion without doubt.

[54] *Stephen takes a very pragmatic view.*

SC: Doubt isn't the opposite of faith, doubt is part of faith. And on a good day my trust, you know, fills me with a kind of joyful compulsion to do the things of God. And on a dark day sometimes my doubts rise to the surface and I feel, you know, sometimes very distant from God. So, I don't think about faith as being big or small – and I think that's probably what Jesus means. He just says, 'well, look, you know, who cares about – size doesn't matter when it comes to faith.' He says, you know, 'the tiniest, tiniest bit of faith is enough.' And a little bit of trust goes a very, very long way. So I just simply accept that doubt is real – it's a part of faith. Therefore it's not so much that I don't worry about it, but I don't expect it to be otherwise.

[55] David goes back to basics.

DW: I play golf – very badly, at times. And the thing about golf is that with the advice of other people, and trying to self-correct during a round of golf if everything's going wrong, you can get yourself into the most oddest of positions. And sometimes in sport – and particularly golf – you just have to say, 'am I doing the basic things right? Am I keeping my eye on the ball?' Once you get the basic things right, things begin to follow. And so for me, I ask the question, 'am I saying my prayers? Am I reading my Bible? Am I going to church? And am I witnessing to other people about my faith?' If I'm trying to do those, kind of, basic things, then often I find that faith grows, develops, works its way out.

[56] I took the opportunity to ask Stephen if he had any Bible passage that he can turn to for strength when he's under pressure. It's the Psalms!

SC: What I like about the Psalms is that you can never outdo them. If you're feeling angry, you're never as angry as the Psalms. If you're feeling joyful, you're never as joyful as the Psalms. If you're racked with doubt, you're never as filled with doubt as with the Psalms. You know, the Psalm is, kind of – always, always trumps you and therefore, kind of, gives you words to express your own expressionless feelings – whether they be of joy or sorrow or anger or passion – or whatever. And therefore they're very permissive. You know, sometimes I think we wonder, you know, is it all right as a Christian to feel this angry with God – or this filled with doubt, or this sorrowful? Well I say, you know, read the Psalms and that tells you that, you know, within Scripture itself God has given a voice to our deepest, deepest feelings. So I guess, yes, that's probably the book of the Bible I turn to the most.

[57] David Winter ends the course booklet by reminding us that God isn't remote and distant. In Jesus' language he is 'Abba', the Heavenly Father of the Lord's Prayer. I asked Shirley and Stephen if they found this a helpful title for God. Different answers.

SW: Not completely. It's trying to understand God as omnipotent that gives me some very vague insight into the Almighty. It's not so much God as father. I think that the relationship, in terms of describing it through human relationships, for me is almost always Jesus Christ. And God remains an extraordinary kind of force. So, no, I don't think I respond well to that. I think I do think of God as being utter – very, very different from a human being – and Christ as being the combination of the two.

SC: I got a wonderful invitation from the local Muslim community here in Chelmsford to speak to them on the birthday of the Prophet Muhammed. And it was a, you know, wonderful, gracious invitation – and they asked me to speak to them about the spirituality of Jesus Christ. And I began my little address by saying, 'the spirituality of Jesus Christ can be summed up in one word, and that word is "Abba". That Jesus called God "Daddy"'. And, of course it sums up a revolution in the way that we think about God, and a revolution in the way we think about our relationship with God. That God, whatever you think about him now, God is not the far off, distant, removed, remote, dictatorial type of God, he's the here-and-now, intimate – this is the word the child uses when she climbs into her father's lap. Daddy. It's a shocking word. Shocking for the translators of the Bible into English. They couldn't use it. A bit shocking for us today even, that you know – are we that intimate with God? Well, let me give you another example of that intimacy. Here we are sitting, talking, recording all this for the York Courses. I've set aside a couple of hours in my diary for you. Who has the right to break into this meeting and disturb me? Well, I hope nobody. My secretary will be very good at, you know, making sure that nobody will come and disturb us. But it is just possible that one of my children might come through the door. They don't have to make an appointment to see me. I hope they knock – I have tried to train them to knock on the door if it's closed, but even so, they have that relationship with me that means they don't have to book an appointment in my diary to see me, even though I am this very, very busy person. It's a different relationship that they have, to anybody else. And that's the relationship we have with God. And the whole of Jesus' spirituality is summed up in that radically intimate relationship that he has with the Father – and he says is now open to each and every one of you.

[58] *And finally, Lucy Winkett reflects for us and offers her thoughts on the God who calms our fears.*

It's one of the most often repeated expressions in Scripture, 'Don't be afraid'. Angels say it, Yahweh says it through the prophets, Jesus of Nazareth says it: 'don't be afraid.' In fact it appears 365 times – one for each day of the year. But fear is a good thing sometimes – our instincts tell us when we are in danger, or when we are under threat. I serve currently at a church in central London; and one of our staff was threatened by a man who was a drug user; he came at him with a needle. His fear at that point was very important: and gave him energy to run faster than his assailant and run away. And Scripture isn't just full of reassuring words about not being afraid. The fear of the Lord is the beginning of wisdom. If we're able to live our lives as prayer in themselves; an attitude, an orientation, a letting-go of our own egos to rest in God, then we will avoid a God who calms our fears becoming a kind of 'easy listening' God; a God who smoothes everything over, makes it all better and sings us to sleep. The truth is that God doesn't always calm our fears; neither should they be calmed; but a re-orientation of our lives will mean that all the trivial things of which we're afraid: what people think of us, how we're doing compared with others and so on; all these become gradually more unimportant and our fear is slowly replaced with deep and lasting trust in the one who has loved us from the beginning.

The Course Booklet ...

... is written by **CANON DAVID WINTER**, former Head of Religious Broadcasting at the BBC. He is a prolific author and a popular broadcaster, well known from his contributions to Radio 4's *Thought for the Day*.

ISBN 978-0-9557437-9-5

9 780955 743795

ISBN 978-0-9557437-9-5

YORK COURSES

York Courses
PO Box 343
York YO19 5YB UK
T: 01904 466516
www.yorkcourses.co.uk
E: info@yorkcourses.co.uk

PARTICIPANTS on the CD/AUDIOTAPE

The Rt Hon. Professor SHIRLEY WILLIAMS (Baroness Williams of Crosby PC) is a British politician, academic and author. Co-founder of the Liberal Democrats, and a member of the House of Lords since 1993, she is also Professor Emeritus of Elective Politics at Harvard University. A Roman Catholic, Shirley Williams attends church regularly, often with her grandson.

BISHOP STEPHEN COTTRELL – was appointed Bishop of Chelmsford in 2010. Before ordination he worked in the film industry, and for a year at St Christopher's Hospice in Sydenham. A member of the Governing Body of the College of Evangelists, he is the author of numerous books.

REVD PROFESSOR DR DAVID WILKINSON – a Methodist minister and Principal of St John's College, University of Durham, David has Ph.Ds in astrophysics and theology. He is an author and regular contributor to Radio 2's *Pause for Thought* and Radio 4's *Prayer for the Day*.

REVD LUCY WINKETT – Rector of St James's Piccadilly, previously Precentor at St Paul's Cathedral. She was the author of Archbishop Rowan Williams' Lent Book *Our Sound is Our Wound* and writes and broadcasts on themes of culture, religion, music and gender. She is a regular contributor to Radio 4's *Thought for the Day*.

DR DAVID HOPE introduces the course. He was Archbishop of York from 1995 to 2005. On 'retirement' he took up the post of Parish Priest of St Margaret's, Ilkley. Now retired, he continues to live in his beloved Yorkshire Dales. In 2005 Fr David was awarded a life peerage.

CANON SIMON STANLEY Co-founder of *York Courses* interviews the participants. He is Vicar of St Chad's, a Canon of York Minster and a former BBC producer/presenter.

Printed by The Max Design & Print co. York